Dear Friend,

I am pleased to send you this copy of *Passion With a Purpose*, a 40-day devotional for Easter, with writings by my father, my sister Anne Graham Lotz, and others.

As you read this booklet, I pray you will "*grasp how wide and long and high and deep is the love of Christ*" (Ephesians 3:18, NIV).

For more than 60 years, the Billy Graham Evangelistic Association has worked to take the Good News of Jesus Christ throughout the world by every effective means, and I'm excited about what God will do in the years ahead.

We would appreciate knowing how our ministry has touched your life. May God richly bless you.

Sincerely,

Franklin Graham
President

If you would like to know more about our ministry, please contact us:

**IN THE U.S.:**
Billy Graham Evangelistic Association
1 Billy Graham Parkway
Charlotte, NC 28201-0001
billygraham.org
info@bgea.org
Toll-free: 1-877-247-2426

**IN CANADA:**
Billy Graham Evangelistic
  Association of Canada
20 Hopewell Way NE
Calgary, AB T3J 5H5
billygraham.ca
Toll-free: 1-888-393-0003

# Hope

*for   Each Day*

*Words of Wisdom and Faith*

# Billy Graham

# The Answer to Fear

*Do not be afraid.*
MATTHEW 28:10

Months after the September 11, 2001, terrorist attacks on New York and Washington, psychiatrists reported that people who lived thousands of miles away from those tragic events were still coming to them, unable to sleep and paralyzed by fear. We live in a world shaken by fear, apprehension, and anxiety.

What is the answer to this stifling fear? After Jesus had been put to death His disciples huddled in fear behind closed doors, filled with uncertainty and despair. But suddenly they found themselves in the presence of their living Lord, and at His first words their fears disappeared: "Peace to you" (Luke 24:36). The answer to our individual fears is found in a personal faith in the living, glorified Lord.

And the answer to collective fear is a corporate faith in the living, glorified Lord. The answer to national and international tensions and fears is for the world to know Him who is alive forevermore. We do not worship a dead Christ. We worship a risen Christ, who has broken the power of sin and death and Hell and is alive forevermore. Why then should we fear?

# Christ Is Risen

*He is not here, but is risen!*

LUKE 24:6

Easter Sunday is the most triumphant and joyous day in the calendar of the Christian Church—and it should be!

For many people the resurrection of Jesus Christ is symbolized by new Easter clothes, or the bright color of daffodils and beautiful, white Easter lilies. But most of all, the wonder of His resurrection is symbolized in the hope that beats in the hearts of believers everywhere as they sing triumphantly: "Christ the Lord is risen today."

It is the message "Jesus is alive!" that lifts Christianity out of the category of dead superstitions and archaic religions and makes it the abiding faith of millions. The angel's message is true: "He is not here, but is risen!" And now God's promise is for you: "If you confess with your mouth the Lord Jesus and believe in your heart that God has raised Him from the dead, you will be saved" (Rom. 10:9).

# A Purpose and a Power

*Go quickly and tell . . .*
*that He is risen from the dead.*

MATTHEW 28:7

When Samuel Morse, inventor of the telegraph, sent his first message, he telegraphed these words: "What hath God wrought!"

The greatest news ever sent tells of a far greater event God has wrought: Christ is risen. On that first resurrection day the angel at the tomb delivered the most important message anyone can ever hear: "He is not here; for He is risen" (Matt. 28:6).

When Adam and Eve first sinned, God's warning became a reality: "You shall surely die" (Gen. 2:17). From that moment on, death reigned over the human race—and with it fear, dread, and superstition.

But Christ's resurrection changed all that, bringing hope and salvation to all who put their trust in Him. Listen: Death is a defeated foe! Christ has won the victory. That is why Paul could say, "Thanks be to God, who gives us the victory through our Lord Jesus Christ" (1 Cor. 15:57). Is your confidence in Jesus Christ, the risen Lord?

# He Suffered for You

*His visage was marred more than any man.*

ISAIAH 52:14

When Jesus Christ was on the Cross, His blood draining the life from His body, He knew what it was like to be alone and wracked with pain. But Jesus' pain was far more than just physical pain, for He was suffering God's judgment on all the sins of the ages—the greatest darkness of the soul ever known. As the divine Son of God, He was perfect and without sin. But all our sins were placed on Him, and He took the judgment and Hell we alone deserve. He died in our place.

Why did Jesus suffer? For you. For me. That we might have eternal life and have His peace in the midst of life's storms. That we might know that He understands our pain and suffering and stands ready to help.

Why did Jesus suffer? Because God loves us. Because God loves *you*, and Christ willingly went to the Cross for *you*. There was no other way for sin's penalty to be paid, and for us to be redeemed. The Cross is the measure of God's love.

How will *you* respond to His love, poured out on the Cross for *you?*

# It Is Finished

*He was wounded for our transgressions.*

ISAIAH 53:5

On a hill overlooking the harbor of Macao, Portuguese settlers built a massive cathedral. But over time it fell in ruins, except for one wall. On the top of that high, jutting wall, challenging the elements down through the years, was a huge bronze cross.

It is said that when Sir John Bowring saw it, he was moved to write those words familiar to us all: "In the cross of Christ I glory, / Tow'ring o'er the wrecks of time." . . .

When Jesus lifted up His voice and cried, "It is finished," He did not mean His life was ebbing away or God's plan had been foiled. Though death was near, Jesus realized the last obstacle had been hurdled and the last enemy destroyed. He had successfully and triumphantly completed the task of redemption. With the words, "It is finished," He announced that Heaven's door was open.

Kingdoms and empires come and go, but the Cross and all it stands for will always remain, "Tow'ring o'er the wrecks of time."

# The Resurrection and Life

*He who believes in me will live,*
*. . . and . . . will never die.*

JOHN 11:25–26, NIV

We have three great enemies: sin, Satan, and death. Because Christ rose from the dead, we know that sin and death and Satan have been decisively defeated. And because Christ rose from the dead, we know there is life after death, and that if we belong to Him we need not fear death or hell.

Jesus said, "I am the resurrection and the life. He who believes in me will live, even though he dies; and whoever lives and believes in me will never die" (John 11:25–26, NIV). He also promised, "If I go and prepare a place for you, I will come back and take you to be with me that you also may be where I am" (John 14:3, NIV).

How hopeless our lives would be if these words were not true. Every cemetery and every grave site would be a mute witness to the futility and despair of human life. But His words are true! By God's power Jesus rose from the dead and hundreds became witnesses to His resurrection (see 1 Cor. 15:1–8).

What a glorious hope we have because Jesus is alive!

# The Message of Easter

*He has risen! He is not here.*

MARK 16:6 NIV

The message of Easter is the central focus of Christianity.

The Apostle Paul said, "If Christ has not been raised, your faith is futile; you are still in your sins" (1 Cor. 15:17, NIV). It is as simple as that. If Christ is still dead, then He cannot be our Savior, for He was not the Son of God, and He died like all men. More than that, Heaven's doors are still locked.

But if Christ is risen, as the Scriptures teach and as hundreds of witnesses testified (none of whom ever recanted that testimony despite threats and death for many of them), then we have the ultimate hope of humanity—eternal life with the God who made us and the certainty of life beyond the grave.

What does Easter mean to you? It should mean everything, because Christ has conquered death! And that makes all the difference—now and forever!

# Why Did He Die?

*The message of the cross . . .*
*is the power of God.*

1 CORINTHIANS 1:18

We can never grasp the horror of human sin until we realize it caused the Son of God to be crucified. Not Pilate, not Judas, not the mob—but sin.

The ravages of war and poverty, the wrenching pain of loneliness and rejection. The haunting cry of the orphan and widow, the dying gasps of the world's starving—these and a thousand other tragedies all bear witness to the fact that we live in a world poisoned by sin.

And that is why Jesus died. The terrible, bitter cup of humanity's sin sent Him to the Cross. Jesus prayed in those last hours, "O, My Father, if it is possible, let this cup pass from Me; nevertheless, not as I will, but as You will" (Matt. 26:39). There was no other way. Why did He drink that awful cup? So you and I would not have to.

Sin is the second most powerful force in the universe, for it sent Jesus to the Cross. Only one force is greater—the love of God.

# GRACE
## FOR THE MOMENT

*Inspirational
Thoughts for Each Day
of the Year*

# Max Lucado

# Because of His Gift

*I want to know Christ and the power that raised him from the dead. I want to share in his sufferings and become like him in his death.*

PHILIPPIANS 3:10

Trace the path of this Savior, the God who swapped heavenly royalty for earthly poverty. His bed became, at best, a borrowed pallet—and usually the hard earth. He was dependent on handouts for his income. He was sometimes so hungry he would eat raw grain or pick fruit off a tree. He knew what it meant to have no home. He was ridiculed. His neighbors tried to lynch him. Some called him a lunatic. His family tried to confine him to their house. His friends weren't always faithful to him.

He was accused of a crime he never committed. Witnesses were hired to lie. The jury was rigged. A judge swayed by politics handed down the death penalty.

They killed him.

And why? Because of the gift that only he could give.

*The Applause of Heaven*

# The Cloak of Humanity

*Jesus took Peter, James,*
*and John with him, and he began*
*to be very sad and troubled.*

MARK 14:33

"During the days of Jesus' life on earth, he offered up prayers and petitions with loud cries and tears to the one who could save him from death" (Heb. 5:7).

My, what a portrait! Jesus is in pain. Jesus is on the stage of fear. Jesus is cloaked, not in sainthood, but in humanity.

The next time the fog finds you, you might do well to remember Jesus in the garden. The next time you think that no one understands, reread the fourteenth chapter of Mark. The next time your self-pity convinces you that no one cares, pay a visit to Gethsemane. And the next time you wonder if God really perceives the pain that prevails on this dusty planet, listen to him pleading among the twisted trees.

*No Wonder They Call Him the Savior*

# The Standard

*We are made holy through*
*the sacrifice Christ made in his body*
*once and for all time.*

Hebrews 10:10

Only the holy will see God. Holiness is a prerequisite to heaven. Perfection is a requirement for eternity. We wish it weren't so. We act like it isn't so. We act like those who are "decent" will see God. We suggest that those who try hard will see God. We act as if we're good if we never do anything too bad. And that goodness is enough to qualify us for heaven.

Sounds right to us, but it doesn't sound right to God. And he sets the standard. And the standard is high. "You must be perfect, just as your Father in heaven is perfect" (Matt. 5:48).

You see, in God's plan, God is the standard for perfection. We don't compare ourselves to others; they are just as fouled up as we are. The goal is to be like him; anything less is inadequate.

*He Still Moves Stones*

# A Few More Scenes

> *"In [this] world you will have*
> *tribulation," Jesus promises, "but be*
> *of good cheer, I have overcome the world."*
>
> JOHN 16:33 NKJV

God has kept no secrets. He has told us that, while on this yellow brick road [of life], we will experience trouble. Disease will afflict bodies. Divorce will break hearts. Death will make widows and devastation will destroy countries. We should not expect any less. But just because the devil shows up and cackles, we needn't panic.

Our Master speaks of an accomplished deed. . . . "It is finished" (John 19:30). The battle is over. Be alert. But don't be alarmed. . . . The manuscript has been published. The book has been bound. Satan is loosed for a season, but the season is oh-so-brief. . . . Just a few more scenes, just a few more turns in the road, and his end will come.

*When Christ Comes*

# One Incredible Plan

*He humbled himself and was fully obedient to God, even when that caused his death—death on a cross.*

PHILIPPIANS 2:8

When human hands fastened the divine hands to a cross with spikes, it wasn't the soldiers who held the hands of Jesus steady. It was God who held them steady. Those same hands that formed the oceans and built the mountains. Those same hands that designed the dawn and crafted each cloud. Those same hands that blueprinted one incredible plan for you and me.

Take a stroll out to the hill. Out to Calvary. Out to the cross where, with holy blood, the hand that placed you on the planet wrote the promise, "God would give up his only Son before he'd give up on you."

*Six Hours One Friday*

# A Meeting of Moments

*[They] put him to death by nailing*
*him to a cross. But this was God's plan*
*which he had made long ago.*

ACTS 2:23

The cross was no accident.

Jesus' death was not the result of a panicking cosmological engineer. The cross wasn't a tragic surprise. Calvary was not a knee-jerk response to a world plummeting toward destruction. It wasn't a patch-up job or a stop-gap measure. The death of the Son of God was anything but an unexpected peril.

No it was part of an incredible plan. A calculated choice.

The moment the forbidden fruit touched the lips of Eve, the shadow of a cross appeared on the horizon. And between that moment and the moment the man with the mallet placed the spike against the wrist of God, a master plan was fulfilled.

*God Came Near*

# You Were in His Prayers

*Then Jesus went about a
stone's throw away from them.
He kneeled down and prayed.*

LUKE 22:41

The final prayer of Jesus was about you. His final pain was for you. His final passion was for you. Before he went to the cross, Jesus went to the garden. And when he spoke with his Father, you were in his prayers. . . .

And God couldn't turn his back on you. He couldn't because he saw you, and one look at you was all it took to convince him. Right there in the middle of a world which isn't fair. He saw you cast into a river of life you didn't request. He saw you betrayed by those you love. He saw you with a body which gets sick and a heart which grows weak. . . .

On the eve of the cross, Jesus made his decision. He would rather go to hell for you than go to heaven without you.

*And the Angels Were Silent*

# Tipped Scales

*Christ's love is greater than anyone*
*can ever know, but I pray that you*
*will be able to know that love.*

EPHESIANS 3:19

It wasn't right that spikes pierced the hands that formed the earth. And it wasn't right that the Son of God was forced to hear the silence of God.

It wasn't right, but it happened.

For while Jesus was on the cross, God sat on his hands. He turned his back. He ignored the screams of the innocent.

He sat in silence while the sins of the world were placed upon his Son. And he did nothing while a cry a million times bloodier than John's echoed in the black sky: "My God, my God, why have you forsaken me?"

Was it right? No.
Was it fair? No.
Was it love? Yes.

*The Applause of Heaven*

# ANNE GRAHAM LOTZ

MEDITATING DAILY ON GOD'S WORD

## THANK HIM NOW

*He was pierced for our transgressions,*
*he was crushed for our iniquities.*

ISAIAH 53:5, NIV

Perhaps thinking to satisfy the crowd's thirst for blood without actually going so far as to execute Jesus, Pilate had Him flogged. History records that flogging victims either passed into unconsciousness, went insane, or died. The miracle is not that Jesus survived the whipping, but that *He submitted to it!* How easy it would have been for Him to defy them and, without cursing but in righteous judgment, send them all to hell!

Why? *Why* would God allow His Son to endure such physical torture? The answer had been given years earlier, when Isaiah solemnly prophesied, "Surely he took up our infirmities and carried our sorrows. . . . He was pierced for our transgressions, he was crushed for our iniquities; the punishment that brought us peace was upon him, and by his wounds we are healed" (Isa. 53:4–5, NIV).

*Just Give Me Jesus*

## CARRYING THE CROSS

*"Anyone who does not carry his cross
and follow me cannot be my disciple."*

LUKE 14:27, NIV

Imagine what it would have been like to be
Simon, and to have carried the cross of Christ while
following Him up Calvary.

What would it have been like to have shared in
the humiliation of rejection as He was cast
out of the city?

What would it have been like to have felt the
sticky warmth of His blood from the cross
on your skin?

What would it have been like to have felt the
encroaching horror as the place of execution
neared?

What would it have been like to have seen the
executioners who stood waiting impassively
with hammers in hand?

What would it have been like to have the burden
of the cross lifted from your back as someone
said, "This is His cross; you're free to go
now," and He was nailed to it, not you?

*Just Give Me Jesus*

# CLOTHED IN HIS RIGHTEOUSNESS

*And when they crucified Him,*
*they divided His garments, casting lots for them*
*to determine what every man should take.*

MARK 15:24, NKJV

---

When Jesus finally arrived at the place of execution around nine o'clock in the morning, if His treatment followed standard procedure in those days, He was stripped of all His clothes. Possibly He was allowed to retain a loincloth.

Yet because Jesus was stripped "naked," you and I can be clothed! The Bible tells us that all of our righteousness, including the very best things we ever do, are so permeated with sin and selfishness that they are like filthy rags in God's sight (Isa. 64:6). But at the cross, Jesus gave us His perfect, spotless robe of righteousness and took our filthy garments of sin in exchange (Phil. 3:9). On Judgment Day, you and I will be dressed in His righteousness before God because He wore the filthy garments of our sin. We will be clothed because He was stripped!

*Just Give Me Jesus*

## HE WILL FORGIVE YOU

*"Forgive us our debts, as we forgive our debtors."*

MATTHEW 6:12, NKJV

Jesus, the Lamb of God, God's own Son, was sacrificed on the altar of a wooden Roman cross.

Normally, crucifixion victims cursed and screamed obscenities and even passed into unconsciousness from the initial pain. Jesus reacted in a stunningly different way—He prayed, "Father, forgive them, for they do not know what they are doing" (Luke 23:34, NIV). Fifty days later when Peter preached at Pentecost, Jesus' prayer was answered when some of the very men who crucified Him repented of their sins, placed their faith in Him, and were baptized in His Name!

If God could forgive the men who nailed His Son to the cross, why do you think He won't forgive you?

*Just Give Me Jesus*

DAY 21

## GOD'S COMFORT

*Blessed be the . . . God of all comfort,*
*who comforts us in all our tribulation.*

2 CORINTHIANS 1:3–4, NIV

How could Mary bear to watch her Son tortured? Yet how could she tear herself away?

Her entire body must have quivered as though from an electric shock as she heard Jesus calling to her from the cross. Surely her breath caught as she strained to hear His words, yet He spoke clearly, "'Dear woman, here is your son,' and to the disciple [John], 'Here is your mother.' From that time on, this disciple took her into his home" (John 19:26–27, NIV). And somehow, even with the horror of the scene before her, and the weight of agony pressing against her chest, she knew everything was going to be all right. She didn't understand, but in the midst of the anguish only a mother knows as her heart is shattered by the pain of her child, a quiet peace must have stolen its way within when God spoke directly and personally to her from the cross. God had singled her out, He had noticed her, He had cared for her, and she was comforted.

*Just Give Me Jesus*

## BECAUSE HE LIVES

*"I am the good shepherd.*
*The good shepherd gives His life for the sheep."*

JOHN 10:11, NKJV

Real meaning to your life is found in the glorious dawn of God's story, which breaks into full revelation in the Person of Jesus Christ. What an astounding truth! What a life-changing message!

Because He emptied Himself of all but love, you can be filled.

Because His body was broken, your life can be whole.

Because He was forsaken, you will never be alone.

Because He was buried, you can be raised.

Because He reached down to you, you don't have to work your way up to Him.

Because His promises are always true, you can have hope!

Praise God for just giving us Jesus!

*God's Story*

DAY 23
## THE EXCHANGE

*By grace you have been saved through faith,*
*and that not of yourselves; it is the gift of God,*
*not of works, lest anyone should boast.*

EPHESIANS 2:8–9, NKJV

On the hill of Golgotha, when Jesus was stripped of His physical clothes, the execution squad of soldiers divided what little He had between them—His belt, sandals, and other things. But when it came to His beautifully woven inner garment, they decided that instead of tearing it into four pieces, they would gamble for it. So while Jesus hung slightly above them, groaning in excruciating pain, they callously ignored Him and tossed the dice. (John 19:23–24)

People today still toss the dice for the robe of His righteousness. While coldly ignoring His death on the cross, they gamble for His "robe" by betting their eternal lives on the chance that they can earn acceptance with God through their religiosity, or their sincerity, or their morality. But the only way to obtain it is to exchange your sin for it at the cross.

*Just Give Me Jesus*

## STAND UP FOR JESUS

*Joseph of Arimathea asked Pilate for the body of Jesus.*
JOHN 19:38, NIV

Because Jesus had just been executed as a criminal and an enemy of Rome, Joseph's request was exceedingly bold. As a prominent member of the religious community, he ran the risk of provoking not only Pilate but also the other Jewish leaders.

Joseph's action was especially astounding since previously he had been so timid and fearful of the opinions of others that he had kept his belief in Jesus as the Messiah a secret. Now, however, he came out of the closet and "with Pilate's permission, he came and took the body." Even more astonishing, "he was accompanied by Nicodemus, the man who earlier had visited Jesus at night" (John 19:38–39, NIV).

The Father's heart must have been deeply moved to see these two fearful, prideful Jewish men throw caution to the wind. They had been silent when they should have spoken. But no more! Now they were standing up for Jesus!

*Just Give Me Jesus*

# Truth

## FOR TODAY

*A Daily Touch of God's Grace*

# JOHN
# MacARTHUR

# The True Picture

*I determined not to know anything*
*among you except Jesus Christ and Him crucified.*

1 Corinthians 2:2

Jesus Christ evokes many images in the minds of people. Some picture Him as a baby in a manger—the Christ of Christmas. Others picture Him as a child, perhaps living in the home of a carpenter or confounding the religious leaders of Jerusalem. Many picture Him as a compassionate and powerful healer who restored the sick and raised the dead. Still others picture a bold and fiery preacher speaking the Word of God to great crowds. And there are those who see Him as the consummate man—a model of goodness, kindness, sympathy, concern, care, tenderness, forgiveness, wisdom, and understanding.

Yet the one image of Christ that surpasses all the rest is Jesus Christ on the cross. To know Christ crucified is to know Him as the author and finisher of your faith—the truest picture of His Person and work.

Christ's suffering on the cross is the focal point of the Christian faith. That's where His deity, humanity, work, and suffering are most clearly seen.

Day 26

# A Suffering Standard

*For such a High Priest was fitting for us,*
*who is holy, harmless, undefiled, separate from sinners,*
*and has become higher than the heavens.*

HEBREWS 7:26

Jesus was executed as a criminal on a cross. Yet He was guilty of no crime—no wrong, no trespass, no sin. He never had an evil thought or spoke an evil word. His was the most unjust execution ever perpetrated on a human being. Yet it shows us that though a person may be perfectly within the will of God—greatly loved and gifted, perfectly righteous and obedient—he may still experience unjust suffering. Like Jesus, you may be misunderstood, misrepresented, hated, persecuted, and even murdered. Yet you must follow His standard.

# Our Sinless Savior

*[Christ] committed no sin,*
*nor was deceit found in His mouth;*
*who when He was reviled,*
*did not revile in return.*

1 PETER 2:22–23

Jesus would have been prominent in Peter's mind when he wrote today's verses because he personally witnessed Jesus' pain—though from afar. In spite of the severity of His pain, however, Christ committed no sin in word or deed.

Isaiah 53:9 says, "He had done no violence." "Violence" is translated as "lawlessness" in the Septuagint (the Greek version of the Hebrew Old Testament). The translators understood that "violence" referred to violence against God's law—or sin. In spite of the unjust treatment He had to endure, Christ did not and could not sin (cf. 1 Pet. 1:19).

Isaiah 53:9 adds, "Nor was any deceit in His mouth." Sin usually first makes its appearance in us by what we say. In Jesus there was no sin, neither externally nor internally.

Jesus Christ is the perfect model of how we are to respond to unjust treatment because He endured far worse treatment than any person who will ever live, and yet never sinned.

# Don't Threaten

*Father, forgive them,*
*for they do not know what they do.*

Luke 23:35

Jesus "did not threaten" in the face of incredible suffering (1 Pet. 2:23). He was spit on, His beard was pulled out, a crown of thorns was crushed onto His head, and nails were driven through His flesh to pin Him to a cross. In any other person, such unjust treatment would have caused feelings of retaliation to well up and burst out, but not Christ. He was the Son of God—creator and sustainer of the universe, holy and sinless—with the power to send His tormentors into eternal flames.

Yet Jesus never threatened His executioners with impending judgment; instead He forgave them. Christ died for sinners, including those who persecuted Him. He knew the glory of salvation could be reached only through the path of suffering, so He accepted His suffering without bitterness, anger, or a spirit of retaliation. May you respond as well to your suffering.

Day 29

# The Weight
# of Our Penalty

*Christ was offered once to bear the sins of many.*

Hebrews 9:28

When the apostle Peter said that Christ "bore" our sins (1 Pet. 2:24), he used a term that means "to carry a massive, heavy weight." That's what sin is. It's so heavy that Romans 8:22 says, "The whole creation groans and labors" under its weight. Only Jesus could remove such a weight from us.

When Christ "bore our sins," He bore the penalty for our sins. He endured physical and spiritual death. When Jesus cried out on the cross, "My God, My God, why have You forsaken Me?" (Matt. 27:46), His was the cry of spiritual death. That was the penalty for bearing our sins.

# The Transformation

*We also should walk in newness of life.*

ROMANS 6:4

The purpose for Jesus' substitutionary sacrifice was that "we, having died to sins, might live for righteousness" (1 Pet. 2:24). Peter doesn't say Christ died so we could go to heaven, have peace, or experience love. He died to bring about a transformation: to make saints out of sinners. Christ's substitutionary work enables a person to depart from sin and enter into a new life pattern: a life of righteousness.

The apostle Paul said, "Our old man was crucified with Him, that the body of sin might be done away with, that we should no longer be slaves of sin" (Rom. 6:6). We have died to sin; thus it no longer has a claim on us. First Peter 2:24 echoes that thought: our identification with Christ in His death is a departure from sin and a new direction in life.

# Christ's Triumph

*Christ also suffered once for sins,*
*the just for the unjust, that He might bring us to God.*

1 Peter 3:18

It's incredible to think that One who was perfectly just would die for the unjust. Pilate was correct when he said of Jesus, "I find no guilt in this man" (Luke 23:4). The charges brought against our Lord were fabricated. The witnesses were bribed, and the conviction itself was illegal.

Yet Christ triumphed through such unjust suffering by bringing us to God. And though believers will never suffer as substitutes or redeemers, God may use our Christlike response to unjust suffering to draw others to Himself.

So when the Lord asks us to suffer for His sake, we must realize we are only being asked to endure what He Himself endured so that we can point others to Him.

Day 32

# A Real Death

*Being put to death in the flesh.*

1 Peter 3:18

Today's verse indicates that Jesus Christ's physical life ceased. Some dispute the resurrection of Christ from the dead by claiming that He never died but only fainted. Supposedly He was revived by the coolness of His tomb, got up, and walked out. But Peter is clear: Jesus was dead—the victim of a judicial murder.

Christ's Roman executioners made sure He was dead. They broke the legs of the thieves crucified alongside Him to hasten their deaths. (A victim of crucifixion could postpone death as long as he could elevate himself on his legs.) However, they didn't bother to break Christ's legs since they could see He was already dead. To verify His death, they pierced His side, out of which came a flow of blood and water—only blood, not water, would have come out if Jesus had been alive (John 19:31–37). Christ was surely dead. And that means His resurrection was real.

# WISDOM

## *for the way*

WISE WORDS FOR BUSY PEOPLE

# CHARLES R. SWINDOLL

# It Is Finished

> *For all have sinned and fall short of*
> *the glory of God, being justified as a gift*
> *by His grace through the redemption*
> *which is in Christ Jesus.*

ROMANS 3:23–24

Stop and think: Upon believing in Jesus Christ's substitutionary death and bodily resurrection, the once-lost sinner is instantly, unconditionally, and permanently "declared 100% righteous." Anything less and we are not righteous . . . we're *almost* righteous.

If we are declared 99.9% righteous, some verses of the Bible would have to be rewritten. Like Isaiah 1:18, which might then read: "'Come now, and let us reason together,' says the Lord, 'though your sins are as scarlet, they will be light pink.'"

Nonsense! The promise of sins forgiven is all or nothing. Eighty percent won't cut it. . . .

When our Lord said "It is finished," He meant "finished."

*The Finishing Touch*

# Amazing Grace

*Fix your hope completely
on the grace to be brought to you
at the revelation of Jesus Christ.*

1 PETER 1:13

Imagine coming to the house of a friend who has invited you over to enjoy a meal. You finish the delicious meal and then listen to some fine music and visit for a while. Finally, you stand up and get your coat as you prepare to leave. But before you leave you reach into your pocket and say, "Now, how much do I owe you?" What an insult! You don't do that with someone who has graciously given you a meal.

Isn't it strange, though, how this world is running over with people who think there's something they must do to pay God back? Somehow they are hoping God will smile on them if they work real hard and earn His acceptance. But that's an acceptance on the basis of works. That's not the way it is with grace.

God smiles on us because of His Son's death and resurrection. It's grace, my friend, amazing grace.

*The Grace Awakening*

# Perfect in Him

> *He has now reconciled you . . .*
> *in order to present you before [God]*
> *holy and blameless and beyond reproach.*
>
> COLOSSIANS 1:22

🌿 Living as we do in a product-oriented culture, we like to package our faith, too. We prefer to sell a slick, shrink-wrapped version of salvation that includes happiness and peace, and happiness here and now, and heaven by and by. While there is nothing wrong with good marketing techniques or teaching principles of authentic success, there is something wrong if we neglect to mention the *process*, which must inevitably include times of defeat and failure.

What I'd like to know is who erected such a happily-ever-after standard of perfection in the first place? God knows very well we aren't able to produce perfection; that's why Jesus, the perfect Son of God, placed us in His family. That's why He gave us a position of perfect righteousness in Him, reminding us by contrast that our own daily experience will constantly fall short.

*Moses: A Man of Selfless Dedication*

# God Takes Care of You

> *Be strong and courageous!*
> *Do not tremble or be dismayed, for the LORD*
> *your God is with you wherever you go.*

JOSHUA 1:15

 Did you know that worry erases the promises of God from your mind. Jesus implies this when He says, "O men of little faith. Do not be anxious then, saying, 'What shall we eat?' or 'With what shall we clothe ourselves?'" (Matthew 6:31) The promise of God is that He will not allow His children to beg bread. He will care for our needs and that's the promise you can claim. Since He took care of our greatest need at Calvary by giving us Christ, then you can be sure He will take care of everything else He considers important for us.

*Perfect Trust*

# Humble in Heart

> *Take my yoke and learn from Me,*
> *for I am gentle and humble in heart,*
> *and you will find rest for your souls.*
>
> MATTHEW 11:29

What is the most Christ-like attitude on earth? Think before you answer too quickly. I am certain many would answer *love*. That is understandable, for He did indeed love to the uttermost. Others might say *patience*. Again, not a bad choice. I find no evidence of impatience or anxious irritability as I study His life. *Grace* would also be a possibility. No man or woman ever modeled or exhibited the grace that He demonstrated right up to the moment He breathed His last.

As important as those traits may be, however, they are not the ones Jesus Himself referred to when He described Himself for the only time in Scripture. . . . "I am gentle and humble in heart . . ." (Matt. 11:29), . . . which might best be summed up in the one word *unselfish*. According to Jesus' testimony, that is the most Christ-like attitude we can demonstrate.

*Laugh Again*

# A Perfect Plan

*He said, "It is finished!"*
*And He bowed His head*
*and gave up His spirit.*

JOHN 19:30

🌺 Though unbelieving men nailed Jesus to His cross, it occurred "by the predetermined plan and foreknowledge of God." It was exactly at the time and in the place and by the means God had determined. And what looked to the eleven confused disciples as mysterious, as well as unfair and unjust (humanly speaking, it was all of the above and more), God looked at it and said, "That is what I've planned. That's the mission My Son came to accomplish."

That's why Jesus' final words from the cross before He died were "It is finished." God's redemption plan had been completed—Jesus' payment for our sin. And then He slumped in death.

*The Mystery of God's Will*

# Stop Running Scared

> *You, O LORD, are a shield about me,*
> *my glory, and the One who lifts my head.*
>
> PSALM 3:3

Did you know that you operate at your poorest when you are scared? A little fear is good for us when danger is present, but a lot of it is demoralizing. It takes away the hope, the dream, the vision, the possibility of overcoming. . . .

Fears lurk in the shadows of every area of life. Perhaps you've suddenly discovered that an unexpected addition to your family is on the way. . . . You may be uncertain where your job is leading. . . . You are uneasy about what's around the corner. Or perhaps you have a doctor's appointment pending and you are afraid of what the exam might reveal. Jesus says, "Stop being afraid. Trust Me!"

Jesus Christ stands at the door. He holds out His hands that are scarred. His feet are pierced, and He bears in His body the marks of death. He says, "I know the pressure you are under. I understand the strain. I know the unfair abuse. But let me offer you some encouragement. Don't be afraid. Look at life through My eyes! Stop letting life intimidate you! Stop running scared. Trust Me!"

*Perfect Trust*

# Make a Difference

*What use is it, my brethren,
if someone says he has faith
but he has no works?*

JAMES 2:14

Does one person make a difference? Let me ask you, did Christ? God so loved the world that He *did something*. He didn't select a committee. He didn't theorize how great it would be for someone to come to our rescue. He didn't simply grieve over our waywardness and wring His hands in sorrow. He did something! And, in turn, the Son of God said to God the Father, "I will go." He *did something* about it. And that's why we can be saved. We don't believe in a theory; we believe in the person of Christ, who died and rose again that we might live and make a difference.

The question is not simply, what do you think of Christ? The question is, what have you done about what you think?

*Esther: A Woman of Strength and Dignity*

# Steps to Peace With God

## 1. God's Purpose: Peace and Life

God loves you and wants you to experience peace and life—abundant and eternal.

### The Bible Says ...

"We have peace with God through our Lord Jesus Christ." *Romans 5:1, NIV*

"For God so loved the world that He gave His only begotten Son, that whoever believes in Him should not perish but have everlasting life." *John 3:16, NKJV*

"I have come that they may have life, and that they may have it more abundantly." *John 10:10, NKJV*

Since God planned for us to have peace and the abundant life right now, why are most people not having this experience?

## 2. Our Problem: Separation From God

God created us in His own image to have an abundant life. He did not make us as robots to automatically love and obey Him, but gave us a will and a freedom of choice.

We chose to disobey God and go our own willful way. We still make this choice today. This results in separation from God.

### The Bible Says ...

"For all have sinned and fall short of the glory of God." *Romans 3:23, NIV*

"For the wages of sin is death, but the gift of God is eternal life in Christ Jesus our Lord." *Romans 6:23, NIV*

Our choice results in separation from God.

People (Sinful)     God (Holy)

## Our Attempts

Through the ages, individuals have tried in many ways to bridge this gap ... without success ...

### The Bible says ...

"There is a way that appears to be right, but in the end it leads to death."
*Proverbs 14:12, NIV*

"But your iniquities have separated you from your God; and your sins have hidden His face from you, so that He will not hear."
*Isaiah 59:2, NKJV*

There is only one remedy for this problem of separation.

## 3. God's Remedy: The Cross

Jesus Christ is the only answer to this problem. He died on the cross and rose from the grave, paying the penalty for our sin and bridging the gap between God and people.

### The Bible says ...

"For there is one God and one mediator between God and mankind, the man Christ Jesus."
*1 Timothy 2:5, NIV*

"For Christ also suffered once for sins, the just for the unjust, that He might bring us to God."
*1 Peter 3:18, NKJV*

"But God demonstrates His own love toward us, in that while we were still sinners, Christ died for us." *Romans 5:8, NKJV*

God has provided the only way ... we must make the choice ...

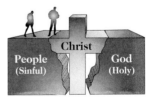

## 4. Our Response: Receive Christ

We must trust Jesus Christ and receive Him by personal invitation.

### The Bible Says ...

"Behold, I stand at the door and knock. If anyone hears My voice and opens the door, I will come in to him and dine with him, and he with Me." *Revelation 3:20, NKJV*

Are you here ... or here?

"But as many as received Him, to them He gave the right to become children of God, to those who believe in His name." *John 1:12, NKJV*

"If you confess with your mouth the Lord Jesus and believe in your heart that God has raised Him from the dead, you will be saved." *Romans 10:9, NKJV*

*Is there any good reason why you cannot receive Jesus Christ right now?*

### How to Receive Christ:

1. Admit your need (say, "I am a sinner").
2. Be willing to turn from your sins (repent) and ask for God's forgiveness.
3. Believe that Jesus Christ died for you on the cross and rose from the grave.
4. Through prayer, invite Jesus Christ to come in and control your life through the Holy Spirit (receive Jesus as Lord and Savior).

### What to Pray:

Dear Lord Jesus,
    I know that I am a sinner, and I ask for Your forgiveness.
I believe You died for my sins and rose from the dead. I turn from my sins and invite You to come into my heart and life.
I want to trust and follow You as my Lord and Savior.
                    In Your Name, Amen.

_____          _____
Date                                            Signature

# God's Assurance: His Word

## If you prayed this prayer,

### The Bible says ...
"For, 'Everyone who calls on the name of the Lord will be saved.'"
*Romans 10:13, NIV*

Did you sincerely ask Jesus Christ to come into your life? Where is He right now? What has He given you?

"For it is by grace you have been saved, through faith—and this not from yourselves, it is the gift of God—not by works, so that no one can boast."
*Ephesians 2:8–9, NIV*

### The Bible says ...
"He who has the Son has life; he who does not have the Son of God does not have life. These things I have written to you who believe in the name of the Son of God, that you may know that you have eternal life, and that you may continue to believe in the name of the Son of God."
*1 John 5:12–13, NKJV*

Receiving Christ, we are born into God's family through the supernatural work of the Holy Spirit who indwells every believer. This is called regeneration or the "new birth."

This is just the beginning of a wonderful new life in Christ. To deepen this relationship you should:

1. Read your Bible every day to know Christ better.
2. Talk to God in prayer every day.
3. Tell others about Christ.
4. Worship, fellowship, and serve with other Christians in a church where Christ is preached.
5. As Christ's representative in a needy world, demonstrate your new life by your love and concern for others.

God bless you as you do.

*Billy Graham*

If you want further help in the decision you have made, contact us:
Billy Graham Evangelistic Association
1 Billy Graham Parkway, Charlotte, NC 28201-0001

1-877-2GRAHAM (1-877-247-2426)
billygraham.org/Commitment